D1029476

RACE CAR LEGENDS

CHELSEA HOUSE PUBLISHERS

RACE CAR LEGENDS

DEMOLITION DERBY

Richard Huff

CHELSEA HOUSE PUBLISHERS
Philadelphia

Frontis: Crash, ram, slam is how it's done in demolition derby, as drivers try to demolish one another's cars and last long enough to come out the winner.

Produced by
21st Century Publishing and Communications, Inc.
New York, New York
http://www.21cpc.com

CHELSEA HOUSE PUBLISHERS

Editor in Chief: Stephen Reginald
Managing Editor: James D. Gallagher
Production Manager: Pamela Loos
Art Director: Sara Davis
Director of Photography: Judy L. Hasday
Senior Production Editor: LeeAnne Gelletly
Publishing Coordinator: James McAvoy
Assistant Editor: Anne Hill
Cover Illustrator: Ian Varrassi

Front Cover Photo: DENT National Championship, Demolition Derby.
   Photographer: Kevin Brown; Drivers: Dan Trent, Jeff Schmidt
Back Cover Photo: Frank Siteman, New England Stock Photo

The Chelsea House World Wide Website address is
http://www.chelseahouse.com

First Printing

1 3 5 7 9 8 6 4 2

Library of Congress Cataloging-in-Publication Data

Huff, Richard M.
   Demolition Derby / by Richard Huff.
   64 p.   cm.—(Race car legends)
   Includes bibliographical references (p.63) and index.
   Summary: Surveys the history of demolition derby competition and types of vehicles, various events, and tactics involved.
   ISBN 0-7910-5416-0
   1. Demolition derbies—Juvenile literature. 2. Automobile racing—Juvenile literature. [1. Demolition derbies. 2. Automobile racing.] I. Title. II. Series.
GV1029.9.D45H84 1999
796.7—dc21
                                              99-31607
                                                  CIP
                                                   AC

CONTENTS

TWISTED METAL, CHEERING CROWDS

"Ten, nine, eight," the excited crowd chants in unison. "Seven, six, five, four, three, two, one, go, go, go!" Within seconds, two dozen brightly painted cars roar into action and start ramming and crashing into one another. It is the start of a smashing, bashing demolition derby, a sport that is attracting more and more fans. At impact speeds up to 20 miles per hour, on what is usually a water-dampened track, cars slam into one another. Drivers have one single objective—render their opponents' cars useless.

Demolition derby is a fight to the end. Its basic idea is simple—elimination through destruction. Whichever car (in some events three cars) is left running at the finish of the mayhem is declared the winner. Usually, however, even the winner is barely operating when the checkered flag, which signals the end, is waved.

The crowd cheers as metal crunches and twists when the cars, alternately driving in forward and in reverse, maneuver to rear-end each other in this 1999 national championship event held in Dunkirk, New York. In a demo derby, drivers often gun their cars in reverse since rear-ending is a favored method of attack. More than 150 drivers competed in this derby.

Each year all across the country, thousands of spectators look forward to counting down the start of these car-bashing events. Held at regular racing facilities, county fairs, and even open fields, a typical demolition derby can draw as many as 60 to 100 cars. The usual scenario is to group participants into "heats," or qualifying events. In a heat, drivers and cars enter the derby area, called the ring, and begin the battle. When, depending on the particular derby, two or three cars are still able to move, the winners from each heat go to the main event, the "feature," the highlight of the derby.

Not all demolition derbies wreck automobiles, however. At times, derby promoters create events around making junk out of school buses, trucks, motorcycles, farm tractors, and even lawn mowers. Other variations of demolition derbies include putting paper bags over drivers' heads so that they can't see what they're hitting and figure-eight competitions in which cars are driven around an eight-shaped track and collide at the intersections. Some derbies have even used compact model cars.

"Demo" cars are not the kind of vehicles parked in driveways or advertised in television commercials, although they look like everyday street cars. Rules allow any hardtop or station wagon but usually not excessively heavy vehicles such as limousines or hearses. Most of the demo cars could be described as "rust buckets." They are mostly the large, heavy cars of the 1970s that have been stripped down and made ready to be banged and slammed and hopefully still run. Often, drivers decorate their cars with crudely painted messages and occasionally mount stuffed animals or signs on car roofs.

There are some rules, however. One strict regulation is that a car number of a specific size must be painted on top of the vehicle. The only qualification for drivers is that they have a valid driver's license. Another rule on most tracks, no doubt to keep the action going, is that one car must hit another every 60 seconds or the car is disqualified. Since drivers smash up their own cars hitting other cars and the idea is to outlast rivals, drivers often try to avoid major crashes.

County fairs are one of the most popular sites for demolition derbies. At the 1998 Erie County Fair in Hamburg, New York, a seemingly endless stream of cars lines up to compete in the qualifying heats and hopefully stay running long enough to enter the big event—the feature.

As one track official explained to an interviewer, "They play possum. They sort of come around and gently glide into somebody. . . ." If that happens too often, a driver gets the black disqualifying flag. Fans want to see action, not timid sideswipes.

The on-track frenzy of 4,000-pound cars hurling at one another, engines roaring, mud flying, and loose car parts littering the tracks is what attracts the fans. In many areas of the country, demolition derbies are a highlight of a week-long county or firemen's fair. In fact, at county fairs, the sport is considered the biggest moneymaking event. In other areas, demolition derbies are regular events held by raceways that normally stage traditional auto racing programs. Although research on attendance is not specific, if the crowds at demolition derbies are any indication, the sport has drawn one of the broadest bases of fans of any form of motorsports. Demolition derbies attract young and old, and men, women, and children.

"I usually run at county fairs and other events, but the fans are a mixed group," said driver Joe Heck, who competes in Minnesota. "The largest draw are the families with children old enough to sit still and watch. The other groups are teenage kids and motorsports enthusiasts. People come to either see their friends drive or watch people simply smash cars as hard as they can."

How did demolition derbies get started? Different stories have circulated about where and when they actually began. The traditional story points to Larry Mendelsohn, a former stock car driver and track promoter at the now-defunct Islip Speedway on Long Island in

New York. According to one version, when Mendelsohn climbed out of his stock car after wrecking in a race, he noticed many of the spectators were more interested in his mangled car than in the race. Mendelsohn, it is said, then got the notion that considering the attention the crowd paid to his wreck, fans might be interested in simply watching cars smash into each other in what might be best called "controlled chaos."

Mendelsohn's first organized event was held at the Islip Speedway in 1961, and during that

Demo derbies are a major attraction that families can share together, and children are among the sport's most eager fans. Enjoying the action at a national championship event are Britanny and Connor Dubé, children of Todd Dubé, a demo driver and president of Demolition Events National Tour (DENT), the national organization that promotes the sport.

decade, his staged mayhem at times attracted more than 14,000 people to watch 200 cars compete for the world championship title. Most of the cars in Mendelsohn's demos were 1955 or 1956 models, and as he explained to *The New York Times* in 1966, "When they come out of a demolition derby, they're through. We've wrecked 74,000 cars in the last five years at derbies in 108 towns and cities."

Other stories put the advent of the sport much earlier. Some say that it began in 1953 when a used car dealer in Wisconsin thought up derbies as a way to get rid of cars that he just could not sell. He decided to smash them up and charge people to watch. Another tale is that the sport was created by racetrack owners who staged demolition derbies at season's end as a way for car owners to get rid of their used racers in preparation for the following season.

All of these stories, however, are contradicted by Demolition Events National Tour (DENT), an organization dedicated to promoting excellence in the sport. Although there are groups that promote derbies on the state or regional level, DENT is the only organization whose scope is national. Each year it produces the National Championship Demolition Derby, the top event in the sport.

According to DENT, its extensive research concludes that the first officially recorded demolition derby actually occurred in 1950 at Hales Corners Speedway in Franklin, Wisconsin. The owner of the track, John Kaishian, has recalled that in 1950 two stock car races were planned at his track. The two race promoters got into a fight, however, and one left, taking some drivers with him. Since not enough cars remained for two races, John came up with another idea: "Why don't we just add a derby show to attract people?"

When the one race ended, some 10 cars rolled onto the track and began slamming into one another. This was more fun than the race, and the fans went wild. As John's wife related, "People used all sorts of ways to promote races and the tracks at that time. Since the first demolition derby was a success, we started to add annual demolition derby events at our track." Ever since, at least two organized demos have been held each year at Hales Corners Speedway, one on Memorial Day and one on Labor Day.

DENT itself is the brainchild of Todd Dubé, its president. As a boy, Dubé watched demolition derbies with his grandfather and father. Carrying on the family tradition of love for the sport, Dubé became not only an enthusiast but an active competitor. In 1996, he won one of the biggest New York State derbies and qualified for the state championship. However, no national level of competition existed beyond the state championships.

Determined to raise the demos to a national level and to bring some standards to a sport that had none, Dubé founded DENT in 1997. To qualify for its annual National Championship Demolition Derby, the only official national event, drivers must finish in the top three at a feature at a demo within the year. DENT offers the largest purse in the sport—$20,000. A winner also receives the official gold DENT Championship Ring and a custom-designed trophy called the Franklin Root Award. The award is Dubé's unique commemoration of

As president of DENT, Todd Dubé (right) has helped boost demo derbies to the national level and is dedicated to setting high standards for the sport. Here, at the 1999 championship event, he presents an award to third-place feature winner Russell Mudget of Holland, Michigan.

the origin of the sport and of a fan. "Franklin" honors the speedway in Wisconsin, and "Root" is a tribute to Dubé's grandfather, Donald Root, who introduced him to the sport.

The sport has come a long way from the day John Kaishian found his inspiration for demos. Demolition derbies drew so much attention that for a time its so-called world championship at Islip Speedway was aired almost weekly on ABC's *Wide World of Sports*, a milestone for any sporting event. As sports shows became more geared to affluent viewers, however, ABC stopped the broadcasts. In 1976, the CBS network did broadcast a one-hour live demolition derby on its *Sports Spectacular* program from Islip Speedway. And during the 1990s The Nashville Network in Tennessee (TNN) aired demolition derby events as part of its regular sports programming.

Although there is some media coverage, and demos have entertained legions of fans since they began five decades ago, demolition derbies have not generated the same kind of nationwide attention as other motorsports. No doubt it does not draw the so-called upscale audience that prefers sports such as tennis or basketball. Its fans may be mostly working-class folks, but they are as dedicated, loyal, and enthusiastic as those for any other sport. For drivers, demos offer the opportunity to enter motorsports without having the huge expenses involved in traditional racing. Still, most drivers, like Todd Dubé, participate simply because they love the sport and have fun doing it.

Although changes have occurred since the first demolition derby event, the heart of the sport remains pretty much the same as it was 50 years ago. Perhaps Mendelsohn summed up the appeal of the sport best when, in 1966, he told *The New York Times*: "We sell danger to the public. But once they get here, it's more humorous than dangerous."

GETTING READY
FOR CRASHING

Aside from the dangers and the fun, one of the main reasons the sport is so popular for participants is the relatively low cost involved to become a driver. To compete in stock car racing, even at the smallest facility in the country, the costs could, and usually do, run into the tens of thousands of dollars. That is just to get on the track for the first time. Thousands more are expended to keep a car running week after week. Ultimately, on the local level, the cost of stock car racing each week far exceeds the amount of money that can be won, making racing more of a sport of love than commerce.

Of course, at the top levels of racing, the economic picture is much different and more profitable. But the reality is that most hopefuls do not make it to the top and spend virtually all of their racing careers on small tracks around the country. For those car and racing enthusiasts unable to pay the

---

Drivers know their cars may not survive a demo in one piece. Nevertheless, they have to prep them. Rules require that although cars may be stripped to the bare essentials—tires, engine, and body—they have to be in running shape and safe for the drivers. On most cars, like this one belonging to Robbie Haught III, who is checking her vehicle, vertical exhaust pipes called "zoomies" stick up from the hood.

17

steep costs in traditional driving, demolition derbies are a way to take part in at least one branch of the race car world. As one demo driver confided to a reporter, "At least, I'm in it."

How much money can be spent on demos? The cost can amount to around a few hundred dollars, more if someone starts from the ground up, and less if an old family sedan is rusting away in the backyard. Most demolition derby vehicles are old two- or four-door passenger cars, which are usually in the last stages of their usable lives. In fact, most of the cars used in today's demos are either dealer trade-ins that could not be sold, cars that were headed for the scrap heap, or vehicles found in junkyards or even along the side of the road. Entry fees at most tracks can range from $10 to $15.

Obviously, demo drivers are not seeking out top-of-the line vehicles. They look for well-built, once-sturdy cars that can still take a licking, hopefully as often as possible. Today's smaller, sleeker, wind-resistant passenger cars are less desirable for derbies, and drivers avoid cars made after the late 1970s. Among enthusiasts, models such as the Chevrolet Impala, the Chrysler Imperial, and the Lincoln Continental are preferred. The rule is the bigger the car, the bigger the blow it can take without stopping. What is perhaps more important is the force of the blow a car can deliver, since the goal is to virtually destroy the other cars. And in a derby, nothing does more damage then the massive fender of a '60s or '70s sedan.

Finding a suitable car is only the first step. A car must then be almost totally converted to withstand the abuse of a demolition derby. In making a vehicle "crash worthy," as drivers

refer to it, they focus on safety and durability. Since slamming cars together at any speed presents danger, drivers modify their cars to create as safe a vehicle as possible and survive the blows from other cars.

Although rules vary from track to track, some basics in the modification of cars are required for any vehicle to compete in demos. Overall, cars must be in decent working order with good brakes. In most states, all glass must be removed from the car, including headlights, side and rear windows, as well as mirrors to prevent injuries from flying glass. Some states allow drivers to remove windshields, although others require that they be left in to protect the driver from airborne auto parts.

All doors must be either held shut with chains or welded shut to keep them from flying off on impact. Hoods and tailgates (on station wagons) must also be securely closed. The interior of the car is just about gutted. Seats, door panels,

The interior of this demo car has been virtually emptied so that parts will not fly loose on impact. For the safety of the driver, only essentials such as the wheel and the battery and gas tank, which are put inside the car, remain. Drivers do wear helmets and use seat belts.

carpeting, and the headliner (the material over the driver's head) are removed to reduce the spread of fire should one break out inside the vehicle. Because rear-end ramming is the preferred method of attack, the gas tank is removed from the back, and a smaller one is put as far forward in the vehicle as possible. The same holds true for the battery, which is often moved from the engine compartment and placed inside the car.

For the most part, drivers are not allowed to reinforce their cars in order to make them more durable in the arena. Some tracks, however, do let drivers add bars to the cars' interiors to reinforce the drivers' compartments. Tracks might also allow a driver to tape a seat cushion between himself and the driver-side door.

Once the car is modified for safety and the ability to withstand impact, then it is painted. Rarely do drivers stay with their cars' original paint. This is the one part of demolition derby in which almost no rules apply, with the exception that the large car number must be visible and no obscene images or phrases are allowed.

In stock car racing, vehicles are usually carefully painted. Because a stock car team has a sponsor who has put up money, the cars typically have the sponsor's logo painted on them. For example, DuPont pays stock car driver Jeff Gordon's team approximately $10 million per year to expose its name to millions of fans.

These standards don't apply in the world of demolition derbies. For the most part, drivers or teams have no sponsors. Since they fund the operations themselves, they can, and do, paint almost anything they like on their cars simply using a can of spray paint. "Hi Mom" and

With the exception of rude lettering or comments, just about anything can be painted on a demo car. Number 131's creative image is mocking, and warning, his rivals with laughter. Other drivers are not always so humorous, coming up with slogans such as "Feel the Vibrations" and "Expect No Mercy."

"Thanks Mom" are common. Nicknames are also popular, such as "The Killer Bee" and "Wild Man Primmy." Others display a driver's intentions with slogans such as "Bad Medicine" and "Death Wish Driving."

Throughout the process of acquiring a car and getting it ready, drivers try to keep their costs down. Very often a car does not last for more than one event, especially for winners who in order to be first may have totaled their cars. When the events are over, drivers are often left with a useless piece of scrap metal. After drivers have stripped any usable parts from their vehicles—engine parts, batteries, gas tanks—it's off to the junkyard to be squashed and recycled as scrap metal.

The Drivers
Behind the Machines

Terry Gullion has been involved in demolition derby for nearly two decades. During that time, he's participated in the sport as crewmember, official, and now as the promoter of demolition derby events in Nebraska. According to Gullion, drivers are drawn to demolition derby for a number of reasons, not the least of which is the low cost of participating. For most, however, he described it as a mix of competition and the pure fun of smashing up cars. "I think for the thrill, excitement, and adventure," he said, reeling off the reasons. "Every day people are out there being careful in not wrecking their own cars. With demos, you can let out all frustrations and have fun at the same time." Gullion added that "Drivers have a no-care attitude. They can just go out there and demolish things for the simple fact that it just doesn't matter."

Demolition derby drivers are not in competitions for the money, which seldom covers the cost of the car and the entry fees. Like Jim Hiltibran, showing off his award for winning a heat at the 1998 DENT championship, most compete again and again. As one driver told an interviewer, "Everybody's a regular. People don't just wake up and say 'Let's crash cars.'"

Anyone with a passion for cars and a valid driver's license can compete in a demolition derby for a relatively minimal amount of money, compared to the cost of entry for other forms of motorsports. And unlike traditional stock car racing, demos provide more opportunities for women to compete and go fender to fender with men. There are no rules against women driving stock cars. In reality, however, women have a much tougher time breaking into traditional racing than do men.

"It's easy for ladies to get into derbies," said Joe Heck, who drives in demos in Iowa. "Around here they have a few lady regulars. Some guys don't feel the ladies should run with the men. But put a helmet on and strap in. What's the difference? The car doesn't know what gender the gas pedal foot is."

Heck should know. His wife also drives in demolition derbies, and they often attend and sometimes compete together. "I run about four demos a year, my wife, Charlene, runs the compact cars one or two times a year," Heck said. "My wife got into derbies by me teasing her, peer pressure, and a motorhead attitude. She likes kicking the guys around. They don't take her serious at first, but they soon learn."

Women have not yet competed against men in the derbies Terry Gullion promotes, but he is not opposed to the idea. Gullion does stage a so-called powder-puff demo for women only, however. "Most of them are drivers' wives," he explained. "They get a lot of pointers from their husbands. They are treated the same as men except we watch for injuries a lot more because the car's already weak and has been in or seen a lot of damage. I do believe that it is easier for women to break into derby than racing. You just don't hear of women going against Richard Petty [top stock car racer] so to speak."

Two women have competed in DENT derbies, however, and others are likely to follow. In 1998, Helen Arnett of Bradford, Ohio, and Jennifer Nuhn, from Ontario, Canada, entered one of DENT's qualifying heats at the Pontiac Silverdome in Pontiac, Michigan. Both had been driving for only two years. During that time, Helen and her Dodge Spirit had won two heats and one feature. With her Chevy Impala, Jennifer had destroyed her competitors in three heats and two features. Jennifer was sponsored by her father.

There is no question that demolition derby is a family affair and a family tradition. Many who participate in the sport got their first taste of demos as children, going to local events with their families. "A great number of my friends and myself all run in demolition derbies," said Pete Sauter, who competes in Minnesota. "We all grew up going to county fairs and watching demo derbies. It looked like so much fun we couldn't resist. As we got older, we either owned or found cars that were either too good to junk or too bad to drive on the road. The obvious answer was to derby them."

Mike Cordeau, another driver who is well known at the derbies, also got his first taste as a kid. The moment he was old enough, he was strapped into a car. "When I turned 18, my parents finally gave me the go-ahead," Cordeau said, admitting that at that age, it

(continued on page 28)

Husband and wife team Tom and Robin Merrell collide as Tom's number 104 rear-ends Robin's number 401. Robin first drove at the Lawrence County Fair when, on the spur of the moment, she decided to participate in a heat, and won.

A Family Tradition

Tom Merrell and his family found themselves lost on a trip in early 1998. While driving along a back road trying to find his way, Tom spotted a 1973 Cadillac DeVille sedan parked in front of a house. Tom was overcome with excitement. "It's perfect," he enthused. The vehicle was exactly what he wanted for his next demolition derby in Pennsylvania. "The guy wanted $500 for it," Tom recalled. "When he found out what I wanted it for, I got it for $250." Tom's passion for demos began when he was a child and went to events with his uncle. When Tom first entered a derby in 1990 and came in third, he was hooked. Since then Tom has competed in 75 derbies, winning more than 20 events.

Demolition derbies are also a family affair for Tom Merrell. Not only do Tom and

The Merrells are a family that "demolishes" together. Proudly posing with one of their cars, Tom and Robin perch on the hood surrounded by their three children in the back and their fathers and mothers in front.

his wife, Robin, drive in demos, but Tom's father and his mother-in-law also compete. Tom's father-in-law helps him weld vehicles between races, and his mother lets him keep from 6 to 10 vehicles on her farm. Robin first participated in a demo derby in 1997 at the Lawrence County Fair in Pennsylvania. She won her heat and joined her husband in the winner's circle. In Robin's fifth demo at the Big Knob Grange Fair in Rochester, Pennsylvania, in 1998, she found herself facing Tom in competition. To continue the family tradition, the couple's 11-year-old daughter, Jennifer, has already informed her mother that she will be entering a demo event in 5 years. "This is a very low budget, family oriented activity," Tom commented.

(continued from page 25)

was highly unlikely his parents would have stopped him.

Since demo competitions are such a family affair, when a family member begins driving, parents, brothers, sisters, uncles, aunts, and cousins all follow their driver to root for him or her. Families also pitch in to help with costs and devote hours to preparing the vehicles for the arena.

Others have become involved in derbies because they had some connection to the sport. As most drivers will admit, the guy who runs the local junkyard may be one of their best friends. Sam Dargo of Indiana, who also competes and is known by his nickname "Slammin' Sammy," was one of them. Working at a junkyard, Sam was surrounded by a seemingly endless supply of cars, many perfect for the crash'em-up world of demolition derby. "I actually got involved out of interest in the sport," Sam has said. "I also tried circle track racing and liked demo derby more."

The relatively low cost of competing is also an important factor. Pete Sauter explains: "I have friends that run stock cars and also run demolition derby cars, but they dedicate most of their time to racing. Most guys I know would love to race, but it's the cost that deters them. I am also one of them. I've helped build race cars, but I can't justify spending the thousands. Derbying is cheaper."

Brian Wynne, who drives in California, likes to think of demolition derbies as the "poor man's NASCAR," referring to the world of professional stock car racing presided over by the National Association for Stock Car Automobile Racing. "You get all the fun and competition of a 'real' motorsport for a fraction of the cost of the crudest circle track race event," Wynne explained.

John Brophy agrees with Wynne. Brophy, a demo driver himself and the president of the Internet Demolition Derby Association, an organization that promotes the sport, points out: "Most [drivers are] guys [who] work in the automotive industry, [as] mechanics, [and in auto] parts stores, but not everybody. It takes very little time, commitment, and resources to have a ton of fun. It's adult bumper cars."

Driving "adult bumper cars" is, despite the destruction, much safer than stock car racing, and injury rates are relatively low. Considering the damage cars inflict on one another, amazingly there are very few cases of serious injury reported. Occasionally, a driver is going to limp from his or her car a little bruised or banged up. It has happened, however, that track workers are hurt. They can be in danger when trying to separate wrecked cars that are hooked and tangled together. In a rare instance, a hunk of flying metal hits and injures someone.

"In ten years, I have seen one broken leg and one broken rib on drivers from particularly brutal hits," Wynne has noted. "The guy with the broken rib duct-taped a pillow to his body and came out to drive in another heat. . . . Safety is the biggest concern with this type of event, accidents are very rare."

Sam Dargo echoes Wynne's observation: "In 18 years of driving, I have never seen anyone get seriously hurt from driving. Whiplash (the sudden flexing of the neck) is common. Occasionally, someone may get cut on a sharp edge in the car."

Fires are relatively rare in demolition derbies. They do occur, however. This driver is making a hasty exit through the windshield area as the car begins to burn.

Fire is also a rare occurrence at a demolition derby. If one does occur, safety crews spread out around the track usually handle the situation swiftly and without injury to the drivers. Tom Merrell recalls an accident he had in 1997. His '77 Chevy Impala exploded during a derby. "It caught on fire," he said. "At first it was smoking so much and I couldn't see the hood. I thought, 'Just one more hit.' Well, it took one more hit and it looked like a bomb going off. The flames were about 25 feet in the air. I wasn't about to stick around; I was out and running." Tom added, "I've never been seriously hurt. It's not nearly as drastic as it looks, although sometimes it is hard to get out of bed in the morning."

The safety record for demolition derby events is in fact a draw for some drivers. Mike Cordeau explains: "I chose the demo over racing because I'd rather go 10 to 15 mph into another car rather than 50 to 60 mph out of turn four [of a stock car race] into a concrete wall."

THE CHEERING
CROWD

Mike Cordeau fondly remembers attending local demolition derbies with his family when he was a child. His father took him to his first event when he was five. Young Mike was immediately drawn to the bruising chaos as vehicles slammed and smashed one another, spinning and squealing their wheels to get in one more lick.

To say Mike was hooked for life is an understatement. "I was a big fan. A big fan!" he exclaims. "Some of the hits the cars would give, the abuse they'd take and seeing people I knew in it was a big thrill." Cordeau, who now drives in demolition derbies, followed the sport closely for a dozen years before he was able to compete. "I knew from the first time I saw it that I was going to be driving in the demo," he said.

Attending a demolition derby is a truly sensory experience. Engines rumble and roar, wheels spin,

While a cheering, yelling crowd eggs him on, Tom Merrell, his car's trunk sprung open, whams a competitor head-on at the Big Knob Grange Fair in Rochester, Pennsylvania. Fans of demolition derbies are loyal, loud, and demand action. The attraction of such destruction draws people to more than 750 county fairs each year as well as to local stock car tracks and national championship events.

the dust thrown up from the tires is like a thick cloud of billowing smoke. And the noise from the crunch of steel on steel is monumental. John Brophy has described his own experience:

> I was amazed at how much a car could bend and still be able to get around. Some of the cars were unrecognizable, but they kept going and going and going. Some bumpers were 10 feet off the ground. Trunks were compacted into the backseat; hoods higher than the roof of the car; and they still smash and smash. All of a sudden the pit gets quiet. Only one motor running. Will the second car get fired up again? A few seconds go by. A fireball pops out from under the hood of the car. Vroom. And it starts all over again.

Motorsports of all kinds are experiencing a rapidly growing popularity, thanks in part to NASCAR's continuing promotion of stock car racing. Although demos have not been widely promoted by the media, devoted fans turn out in droves. Demos got a big boost in the 1990s when The Nashville Network (TNN) aired some events. Even though the network later canceled the telecasts, they had already created an increased national awareness of the sport.

At the local level many demolition derbies are held at stock car facilities. For example, in Belmar, New Jersey, Wall Stadium includes a three-mile oval track built especially for stock car races. However, the track also stages demos several times a year. Because stock car racing is gaining in popularity, so too are demos.

Family attendance at demolition derbies is

encouraged by the fact that many are held on Sunday afternoons, so families can take the kids along. And because the sport is so action packed, children and young people are not likely to get bored. "I think the appeal for the fans is pretty universal," said Brian Wynne. "People will slow down and rubberneck when there's a crash on the freeway. A derby lets us see an hour or two of continuous crashing."

For devotees of motorsports who cannot get to big tracks for races, going to demos is a way of being involved with cars. In some areas, regular demolition derbies at local fairgrounds may be their only up-close contact with any

In a melee of demolition, cars whirl in all directions to crumple and bend one another. This event was a special televised live by the CBS network in 1976. The broadcast came from one of the nation's oldest demo tracks, the Islip Speedway on Long Island, which no longer exists.

Not all of the fun at a demo is car bashing. Drivers and teams get together to talk about their cars, share tips and information, and socialize. At a "pit" party before the beginning of the 1999 DENT derby, a young driver shows off his car.

form of motorsports. "People have long been fascinated with wrecked cars, be it NASCAR crashes or a crash on the highway," said Sam Dargo. "We have a love affair with our cars and when they are no longer of any value to us we have this burning desire to send that Old Faithful car to a fitting end."

Another element of demos' appeal to fans as well as drivers is that feeling of invincibility when one gets behind a wheel. Those super-tanks of the '60s and '70s give drivers the sensation of sitting in a cocoon of steel. They can bash and bang and stop virtually anything that gets in their way. For fans it's a safe way to feel that reckless abandonment everyday life does not provide. And the action in an arena can provide any number of different thrills. "To me stock car races are the same thing over and over," said Terry Gullion. "At a demo, not every time does the same thing happen. Cars don't hit the same [way]. Some cars get put on their side. It's just different every time you have one."

Just as some fans watch hockey games, waiting for slam-bang fights, or some who like to see crashes in stock car racing, some demo fans only relish the mayhem. "It's probably got some of the same appeal of the World Wrestling Federation," said John Brophy. "Actually, it's the same appeal as NASCAR. Who doesn't watch auto racing at least in part to see the cars wreck?"

Brophy is probably right, although the connection has another element. When fans see a crash at a stock car race or a demolition derby, the really exciting and suspenseful part is waiting to answer the question "Will the driver leave the car in one piece?" Luckily, in virtually every instance, the answer is "yes." Fans seem to view demos as human against machine. The more scary the wreck, the louder the cheers when the driver emerges unscathed.

"Spectators love all kinds of auto racing, just like some hockey fans love all sports," said Don Schram, a driver and fan in Michigan. "The appeal is in seeing everyday cars being crushed and destroyed. It's in watching the destruction that shouldn't happen in the outside world. It's seeing a giant car accident again and again and nobody gets hurt."

NERVOUS JITTERS

Pete Sauter minces no words when describing his first experience as a demolition driver. In fact, he is downright blunt about it. "My first demo, probably just like everybody's, was pretty pathetic." These days Sauter is an expert at the sport, but he still remembers that first event. He had bought a Chrysler station wagon from his father, and he knew very little about working on cars. His friends, who were also just beginning, knew as much as he did.

"We thought the bigger the car the better and any station wagon is good," Sauter recalled. "Boy were we wrong." Before beginning his first heat, Sauter went through the list of cars in his event looking for the big models and trying to decide which ones to stay away from. A driver in a Lincoln stuck out as a potential brute to deal with in the arena. "As the afternoon went on, waiting for the start of the derby, I got more and more anxious—butterflies in the stomach—the whole deal," he said. "I was downright

Leaning on his car and grinning broadly, Dan Trent of New Alexandria, Pennsylvania, poses with what is left of his vehicle after a competition. Most drivers admit that no matter how many times they have competed, they still get anxious and jittery before any demo event.

scared by the time I lined up with the other cars and the green flag dropped."

Within a few moments, Sauter had made a few minor hits on other cars and had taken a few hits from others. All the while, he kept his eye on the Lincoln, waiting for the right time to throw his wagon into reverse and barrel into the massive car. When an opening between the cars developed, Sauter saw a clear shot at the Lincoln. As Sauter described it, "I turned around, tried to line up a shot and failed to look ahead at what might come my way. I didn't even get to make a hit on the Lincoln as three cars converged on my front end, destroyed my car and pushed me over the barriers."

A newcomer, Sauter had no spare parts with him. He had to enter a consolation event, a last chance for badly damaged cars that were barely running to make it into the feature event. During the consolation, his car started early and he took a crushing broadside hit. "That finally got me to pull my flag and call it quits," Sauter said. Sauter was not alone with his first-event jitters. Veteran Sam Dargo was so terrified the first time that he felt he needed to go to the men's room. The problem was he had been there once and was already in his car.

Sam Dargo began as a driver after his stint in the junkyard. One day, his boss asked him if he would be willing to drive in a demolition derby using the owner's car. Although Sam had never driven in such an event, he agreed. Sam was going to make his demo debut in a car he and his boss built. Stripping the car of most of its parts, except the windshield, they used what parts they needed from the wrecks on the lot, and put together a vehicle that ran pretty well.

"The night of the derby I was a nervous wreck," Sam remembered. "I had this burning in the pit of my stomach. I was real edgy and quiet. The nervous anticipation was almost unbearable. I rode all the way to the track without saying a word." When a friend who accompanied him asked if he was okay, Sam said yes, but inside he was swirling with emotions.

"Once we arrived at the track, that burning lump in my stomach moved north to my throat," he said. "You would have thought I'd swallowed a tennis ball." Sam calmed himself enough to go to the drivers' meeting, where event officials laid out the rules. Although Sam listened, he was so nervous and focused on getting in the car and driving that he did not really comprehend what was being said. When he walked away, the

Richard "Golden Goblin" Goemaat of Louilia, Iowa, revs his car into action at the 1999 DENT championship. Once inside their cars, drivers find they lose their fears as their adrenaline starts pumping and they focus on winning by demolishing opponents.

At the 1999 DENT derby, Bob Johnen in number 302 is broadsided by Pat Varner. This encounter was not the first hit or first event for either driver. Both are experienced drivers who know how to emerge from the arena in one piece.

only thing he remembered was not to hit other drivers-side doors.

Waiting in the car for the start, Sam felt his legs trembling. The short track appeared to be as wide as three football fields. He was shaking like a leaf as the starter and the crowd counted down from 10 to start. "I left the car in park and gunned the engine," he said. "Realizing I had not put it in reverse, I quickly pulled it out of park. Feet still in tremble mode, I couldn't push the gas pedal."

Sam gathered his wits, however, and soon he was banging into other cars. With each successive hit, his fears were subsiding when suddenly a pink Cadillac rammed him with what felt like a ton of force. "The windshield fell into pieces on my lap. The dash wrinkled like an accordion around my knees. I couldn't move either foot and had my helmet on the driver's side door," he said.

Sam quickly shoved aside the windshield pieces and was able to bend back the dashboard to free his feet. With renewed determination, he kept smashing into the Cadillac until its driver signaled he was done. Revved up now, Sam continued to slam into anything that was moving until no other cars but his were still running. What Sam failed to remember, however, was that he was in a heat event in which the final *three* cars still running qualified for the next race. He had not seen the flagman waving the checkered flag to stop him from bashing the other cars.

Sam's action was a serious breach of the rules, and a few angry drivers came over to chew him out. Sam's friends stopped the confrontation before it got messy while the owner convinced the angry drivers that Sam was a rookie who did not know the rules well enough. They backed off. "I felt like the biggest jerk in history," he said. When emotions cooled down, Sam helped the other drivers make repairs so they could continue with the event. "I made the feature that first time and I didn't do too awful bad," he said. "But I had a great time and knew I would do this again soon."

Most drivers admit that even after years of experience they still get pre-event butterflies. As soon as the metal starts crunching, however, the jitters vanish and adrenaline takes over. "My first demo memory? The first big hit," said driver Joe Heck. "Oh boy, what a rush, the smell of hot motors, hot radiators, smoking tires . . ."

LIFE ON
CRASH DAY

Demolition derby is like any other sport in that a great deal of preparation is required. Before the first fender is twisted or the first tire jumps from its rim, drivers are getting ready behind the scenes. Cars and trailers have to be packed up and driven to the track. Most drivers are at the track hours before the event. They unload their equipment, test their cars, and undergo a pre-event inspection. John Brophy says that when he gets ready for a 7 P.M. demo, his day will start around 10 A.M.

This is how John's day shapes up:

- 10 A.M. packs his tools, spare parts, and the car.

- 1 P.M. starts the drive to the track an hour away.

- 2 P.M. with teammates unloads the car and lines up for pre-event inspections.

- 2:15 P.M. team unloads the parts and tools needed for the event.

Whether a demolition derby is a local, regional, or national event, some basic rules apply to all. Drivers are expected to know the rules and obey them. Here, drivers and their teams assemble to get their instructions before the demolition derby begins.

- 3 P.M. track officials begin selling pit passes and register the cars.
- 3:15 P.M. inspections begin.
- 3:30 p.m. final work begins on the car, including chaining the hood closed, charging the battery, and filling the fuel tank.
- 6:45 P.M. attends a drivers' meeting.
- 7 p.m. drivers line up for a final inspection at which officials check seat belts and helmets.
- 7:10 P.M. crowd counts down to start the race.
- 11 P.M. packs up remains of the car, the tools, and heads home.

On crash day, the basic procedure is much the same at tracks around the country, whether large or small. The entire field of cars, which can range from as few as 20 to more than 200 at national events, is broken down into smaller groups that will run in qualifying heats before the main event. The number of heats depends on the number of drivers who have entered. The more drivers, the more heats.

Event promoters like to have several heats, giving the fans more thrills and also stretching out the event. "Most derbies have two to five heats," says Brian Wynne. "The last three cars running in each heat go into the final heat. But before that is run, most derbies have a consolation or 'hooligan' heat where anyone who can get their used and battered car to run can have a last wild-card shot at getting into the main event." A promoter may also offer more than one division of vehicles—compact cars, trucks,

full-size cars. In that case, each division will have qualifying heats and a feature event.

Between each heat, teams head to their pit areas and work on their cars. Even though cars are still running and able to advance to the feature, they still need repairs and tuning up. "We always require work on the cars between the heats and the feature," said Sam Dargo. "Once you wreck a car, you sometimes have major work to do in a limited time so you can become quite busy. The only time you take a break is when your night is over, when you are out of the competition for the night."

When the event is over, drivers and teams

Their uniforms identify the technical and track officials, whose jobs include inspecting cars for safety and for any violations, laying down the rules, and seeing to it that drivers follow regulations.

After an event, the winners' vehicles are inspected. Officials are looking for any illegal welding of a damaged car. If car parts are welded or chained to secure them, they must all be done the same way so that no one car has a big advantage over another.

face a major decision: What to do with their cars? If a vehicle is still running, or at least salvageable enough to race again, most teams will load up the remains and tow it home. If the car is ready for the junk pile, teams usually strip any working parts that might be of use in the future on another car.

"If they are built right and have experience and good drivers to drive them, they will last," said Terry Gullion. "But you can't get a car at the last minute and get it prepared properly and expect it to last." Brophy agrees. "If the driver feels he can get another race out of it," he explained, "he'll drag it home and fix stuff. If not, he can leave it [at the track] or take it home and strip it and junk it for money." "Reused cars are common," added Brian Wynne. "I would guess that about fifty percent of the new cars that run in a derby will come back again. Usually the things that stop a car are minor: a broken wire or a flat tire."

Among the parts drivers usually hang onto after a car is damaged are the engine and the transmission. "A derby driver does not always need a new car every time," said Pete Sauter. "It all depends on the car's make, model and year and condition before the derby. Also, how hard you hit. I've still got one after two years that will run once or twice more. Depending on where I run, I would say that seventy-five percent of the cars that run that day are junk by the end of the event." More experienced drivers will often take the parts off their irreparable cars and search out junkyards with a similar make and model. As a result, they reduce their investment in the cars they run and salvage more each time.

"After removing batteries, fuel tanks and sometimes special tires and seats, most cars in my area are sold for scrap, with the current rate being $30 to $50," said Don Schram, who drives demo derbies in Michigan. For many the $30 that comes from the scrap sale helps defray the costs of entering the competition.

Each time Mike Cordeau races, the costs are about the same. He spends $20 to enter the event, as much as $200 for the car, although he has spent less, and about $50 to paint it. "Costs of a derby car can vary widely," said Pete Sauter. "I've received free cars, paid as little as $25 and as much as $600. My run-of-the-mill car costs about $100, and probably another $50 to $100 to prep it. The longer you're in the sport the cheaper it becomes since you save parts that you can reuse. I guess you could say we recycle."

Brian Wynne, driving in California, says it costs as little as $250 to run, although he estimates his costs at between $600 and $1,000. Joe Heck from Iowa has a lower estimate. "The average I pay for a car is $50 and adding about another $50 in parts and safety equipment."

Typically, drivers and their teams participate in 5 to 10 events each year, depending on where they live. For instance, Terry Gullion staged 4 events in Nebraska in 1998 and planned on holding 10 in 1999. In Sam Dargo's area, 5 demos are held each year.

Relatively low costs notwithstanding, demolition derby is not a sport in which participants can make a financial killing. Often, drivers pay more to compete than they earn by winning. Some local events can pay as much as $1,000 to the winner, while drivers finishing in 2nd through 10th place share in some purses. But a driver finishing 10th in an event paying $1,000 to win might only get $25. Sometimes, in addition to features, heats can also pay out some money. The winner of a heat could possibly get as much as $100, with the runner-up collecting $50.

There is an exception, however. The DENT annual national championship guarantees a purse of $20,000, the largest in the sport. The

Rumpled and still smudged with grease, a delighted Rick Harrington of Princeton, Wisconsin, proudly displays his DENT Franklin Root Award. Rick won the feature event and championship title in 1998 by making the final hit and being the last car running on the track.

winnings are divided among the first-, second-, and third-place winners. From time to time, DENT also presents various special features in which winnings are also relatively high for the sport. For example, in 1998 demo drivers could compete in a Mad Dog feature in which the competitor judged to be the most agressive driver won $1,000. The same year one budding artist won the Creative Paint Job Award and took home the $1,000 prize.

DENT's 1998 championship event drew 204 drivers from around the United States and Canada. In 1999, 172 drivers from 26 states, including three women, entered the event, held at the St. John Arena in Steubenville, Ohio. The youngest competitor was 18 years old; the oldest was 59. According to DENT, fans numbered some 10,000, and the event was sold out.

Demolition derby fans are possibly the most enthusiastic and vociferous of any motorsports spectators. And DENT gives them a chance to participate by asking them to vote for their favorite drivers in certain special events. Fans vote with the level of their applause. In voting for heat winners at the 1998 championship, the crowd was urged to applaud for drivers who hit the hardest and who put on a good show in trying to demolish their opponents. The instructions were quite specific. Don't vote based on the color of the car, the paint job, or the driver's hometown. And fans were definitely told not to applaud any "sandbaggers"—drivers who park in corners and don't move.

Although DENT draws scores of drivers and thousands of fans and awards generous prizes for the sport, not many drivers are in it for the

Raising his arms in a victory gesture, Scott Zizelman of Celina, Ohio, followed in the footsteps of Rick Harrington when he won the 1999 DENT championship.

money. Since they have to work at full-time jobs, demos are at best a hobby. "The money can be a sore spot," admitted Pete Sauter. "I've been running for 10 years and I'm thousands of dollars in the hole. Despite being on the circuit as long as I have, I'm still learning and finally starting to see trophies and checks."

Running in demolition derbies does return something more than cash, however. "The rewards don't come from the check after the race," said Don Schram. "It's from the crowd during the race. Even over the loud cars and even louder crunches, the drivers can hear the crowd in the stands. There's nothing like the feeling you get when the adrenaline is flowing and you can hear the fans cheering you on."

Joe Heck agrees. "Money? If you're in it for money, you're not going to be in it for long," he commented. "I break even at best. I'm in it for the fun. I love wrenching [working on cars]. Some people hunt animals, I hunt cars." It's no surprise that Heck is not alone. "I don't believe any of us do it for the money," said Dargo. "I think the reason we do it is we are modern-day warriors who accept the challenge of other competitors to do battle. We go out there un-afraid and accept the pain and agony that befalls us and we bask in the limelight of each win. We become somewhat heroes in our localities and the notoriety precedes us to each battlefield."

That "notoriety" is represented in fan appre-ciation. After most events, the crowd is allowed to enter the pit and visit with the drivers and teams. Many times, young children are the ones eager to search out a driver. Fans seem to perceive that the fence separating them from the drivers is a boundary between normal humans and heroes. Once the event is over, the boundary is down, and the typical fan can meet those supermen and women. "The fans are great," said Heck. "The handshakes, the excited voices. But most of all is the kids. I make a note and make time to talk to the neighborhood kids, even let them sign or paint on the cars. They love saying 'Hey, that's my car Joe's driving.' That's the best."

CRASHING INTO
THE FUTURE

Although the popularity of demolition derbies does appear to be growing, the future of the sport is as yet unknown. National promotion by DENT has given demos a boost. Organizations such as the National Demolition Derby Association, which, despite its title, is regional in scope (the Midwest), have also helped increase demos' exposure to the public. The Internet has become part of the demo scene as well. John Brophy's Internet Demolition Derby Association allows fans and others to share tips and ideas and express their opinions.

Still, the reality is that without major television exposure, any sport has difficulty flourishing. The decision of Nashville's TNN network to air a few demolition derby events certainly helped bring the sport some national attention. But in early 1999, the network's *Motor Madness* telecasts were totally

---

Standing on top of his car, unable to contain himself, Aaron Stickley, the winner of the pre-feature 1999 DENT Creative Paint Job competition, excitiedly waves the checkered flag in celebration. Although demolition derby does not get a lot of media attention, it is also not likely to come to an end soon. A solid base of loyal fans and men and women who love to smash and compete are likely to carry demolition derbies well into the 21st century.

canceled and replaced with coverage of a new form of Roller Derby.

Another factor affecting the future direction of the sport is the move by major auto manufacturers to gradually phase out their large, heavy, gas-consuming cars. Following the oil shortage of the 1970s, automakers concentrated on the compacts, and the big, powerful sedans so prized by diehard derby drivers became scarce. Many demo promoters are already anticipating the day when large cars will be a thing of the past. Events are being staged specifically for four-cylinder models such as Pintos, Chevettes, and Tempos as well as for some six-cylinder cars.

"I'm still undecided about the future of the sport," said Pete Sauter. "Compact derbies, mid-sized derbies, and pickup derbies have started around here [in Minnesota], but they haven't gained the attention the full-size car derbies maintain." Sauter expects that a few drivers like himself will still be able to find full-size cars in junkyards. "It's going to be a while before the other styles gain in popularity," he said. "It's most likely to come down to the compact, front-wheel drive derbies. . . . It does seem like the next logical step in derbies, they're plentiful around here and relatively cheap."

Because generally only a handful of demolition derbies are held in various regions of the country, the supply of big cars will likely last a while longer. In addition, automakers have continued to make some form of the giant cars, although in fewer numbers. Chevy manufactured the Impala and Caprice models well into the 1990s. Ford continues to make the Crown Victoria, and there is always the Lincoln Continental. Demo drivers should be supplied with enough vehicles to continue well into the 21st century. And with the boom in sales of sports utility vehicles in the 1990s, it will not be long before they too are being smashed up for fun.

"Most of us in the Internet Demolition Derby Association are looking forward to the sport utility demolition derby," said John Brophy. "That should happen in 15 to 20 years." Brian Wynne actually jokes that demolition derbies are having a positive effect on the environment because "they are accelerating the removal of gas-guzzling road hogs from the streets and empty lots of our country."

A decade ago, drivers expressed that notion as a way to put a positive spin on the sport. Today the idea is a valid reason to applaud the sport. "You will see that many drivers are having a difficult time finding big cars and are going to smaller, newer vehicles," Wynne said.

Mike Cordeau firmly believes that demos are heading in that direction. "The sport up here will eventually be four bangers," he said, meaning the four-cylinder models. "The big cars are pretty hard to find. The hard part about these cars [four cylinder models] is it's hard to make them last more than one heat. You really have to know how to set up and drive these little buggers."

Still, even if the sport moves to smaller cars, mechanical issues will still have to be dealt with. As Brophy has pointed out, the overriding question is whether the modern cars with their plastic parts and electronic components will be able to withstand the abuse of a demolition derby. "One thing that will be certain," he said, "we're all going to have to disarm airbags."

Aside from the vehicle issue, the sport has suffered from something of a negative image

Predictions about the death of demolition derbies seem to be unfounded. Across the country, at local fairs and tracks and at large regional arenas, demo cars like these line up almost weekly to wait for the starter's flag and thrill fans with their crashing, bashing, and slamming.

over the years, just as stock car racing suffered in its early days because it was seen as a sport for the less "respectable." Then national television began promoting drivers as true heroes, and eager sponsors exposed them to the world as their clean-cut, well-spoken representatives. So too, demolition derby is often tossed aside as a sport for the working class. After all, the men and women in demos are not full-time drivers, and the monetary rewards are slim compared to those in stock car racing.

Despite the early negative image of most motorsports, especially with the so-called mainstream public, many have gotten past those perceptions as the sports have grown. Because sponsors will pay millions of dollars to NASCAR teams, stock car racing has spruced up its image. And because NASCAR also commands national media attention, other motorsports are forced to boost their images as well if they are to compete for attention. Demolition derbies do have some limited sponsorship deals, although there is not the pressure to create a professional image. How could there be? Demo vehicles are born to be damaged no matter how hard drivers try not to total them.

How the public perceives demolition derby is changing, and for the better. As a sport with a tradition of involving entire families, it is attracting men, women, and children from all walks of life who want to share their enjoyment with one another. And, the more exposure demos get, the more people they will attract. Sam Dargo has summed it up:

> The sport faces growing pains as any sport. It has been around a long time but it has been more or less considered a low-class, no character type of sport that guys with rotting teeth and dirty clothes are all that would enjoy it. The sport is not that way at all. Perceptions have changed over the last few years and people are starting to realize this is a respectable sport. They enjoy watching the warriors go out with a severe impact and many follow . . . the circuit to each track faithfully like many race fans.

Dargo predicts that as long as cars are being made, there will be demolition derbies.

GLOSSARY

compact car
A small car usually equipped with a four- or six-cylinder engine. Examples are Ford Tempo and Chevrolet Chevette.

consolation
An aspect of a demolition derby in which drivers are given a last chance to get into the main event and compete for the title.

demolition derby
An organized auto event in which drivers smash and crash their vehicles into those of other drivers until only one car has made the last hit and is still running.

feature
The main event, or championship round, of a demolition derby after drivers have competed to be in the feature.

figure 8
A track shaped like the number eight around which cars race and then crash at the point where the lines intersect.

four banger
A car with a four-cylinder engine.

full-size car
A large family sedan, occasionally used as a limousine or official vehicle such as a police car. Examples are Ford Crown Victoria and Chevrolet Impala.

heat
A qualifying event in which drivers compete to gain entry into the main event, or feature.

powder puff
A derby event held only for women drivers.

PHOTO CREDITS:
Craig Melvin/DENT: 2, 6, 14, 16, 27, 30, 36, 38, 41, 42, 44, 47, 53, 56, 60; Todd Dubé/DENT: 9, 19, 21; Kevin Brown/DENT: 11, 22, 48, 51; Robin and Tom Merrell: 26, 32; Photofest: 35.

FURTHER READING

Conniff, Richard. "Crash, Slam, Boom!" *Smithsonian*. January 1999, Vol. 29, No. 10.

Savage, Jeff. *Demolition Derby*. Parsippany, N.J.: Crestwood House, 1996.

Seymour, Tres. Schindler, S.D. *The Smash-Up, Crash-Up Derby*. New York: Orchard Books, 1995.

WEBSITES

www.demo-derby.com
Internet Demolition Derby Association

www.ndda.org
National Demolition Derby Association. P.O. Box 222, Tower Hill, Il 62571.

www.smashcar@msn.com
Demolition Events National Tour (DENT). P.O. Box 349, Lakeview, NY 14085.

ABOUT THE AUTHOR

Richard Huff is an award-winning journalist. His previous books include *Behind The Wall: A Season on the NASCAR Circuit*, *The Insider's Guide to Stock Car Racing*, *The Making of a Race Car*, *The Jarretts*, and *Formula One Racing*. He is a staff writer and motorsports columnist for the *New York Daily News*. His work has appeared in such national publications as *Stock Car Racing Magazine*, *Inside NASCAR*, *Circle Track*, *The Washington Journalism Review*, *Video Review*, and *NASCAR Truck Racing Magazine*. He lives in New Jersey with his wife, Michelle, and son, Ryan.

ACKNOWLEDGMENTS

Special thanks to John Brophy of the Internet Demolition Derby Association, Todd Dubé of DENT, and their respective fellow members without whom this project would not be complete. Thanks also to Michelle and Ryan Huff.

INDEX